GABRIEL FAURÉ

Pièces brèves pour piano
Op. 84

Urtext

Edited by / Herausgegeben von
Roy Howat

ALLE RECHTE VORBEHALTEN · ALL RIGHTS RESERVED

EDITION PETERS
LEIPZIG · LONDON · NEW YORK

CONTENTS

Preface iv
Préface v
Vorwort vii

Piéces bréves pour piano
Op. 84

I	E♭/*mi bémol*/Es-Dur	2
II	A♭/*la bémol*/As-Dur	6
III	A minor/*la mineur*/a-Moll	10
IV	E minor/*mi mineur*/e-Moll	13
V	C♯ minor/*do dièse mineur*/Cis-Moll	16
VI	E minor/*mi mineur*/e-Moll	18
VII	C/*do*/C-Dur	21
VIII	D♭/*ré bémol*/Des-Dur	25

Critical Commentary 31

PREFACE

Fauré's *Pièces brèves* come from vintage years but are still surprisingly little heard, despite their attractiveness and musical quality. Among several factors, they have long been hampered by some problematic metronome markings (an issue addressed in the present edition). Their partial origin as sight-reading pieces makes them slightly easier than many of Fauré's piano works, even if most of them call for the stretch of an adult hand, and they make an excellent introduction to Fauré's piano music for those not already acquainted with the larger pieces.

The collection's size, title and order at first took shape somewhat haphazardly. Probably the first spur was Fauré's composition of a two-page sight-reading test in E♭ for the women candidates in the Paris Conservatoire's end-of-year public examinations in July 1899. (At that time it was still considered proper to give men and women separate examinations.) When the piece was printed in the Parisian daily *Le Figaro* on 29 July 1899, Fauré was already aged fifty-four but had been on the Conservatoire's teaching staff for less than three years. For many years he had been viewed as too dangerously modern for that institution, of which – ironically – he became the director in 1905.

On 3 February 1900 *Le Figaro* again featured Fauré, this time with an unpublished *Feuillet d'album* in A♭. Although plans for the piece were not mentioned there, it must have been around then that Fauré drew up a title page for '*Feuillets d'album, pièces pour piano*' in A♭ and E♭ (the present nos. I and II in reverse order). The E♭ piece is none other than the 1899 test piece expanded to almost twice its original length. (The present Appendix shows the original ending, letting us appreciate Fauré's later additions all the better, not least the ravishing modulations of bars 19–24.) Some time later a '3' was pencilled on the manuscript title page in front of the words '*pièces pour piano*'; the unidentified third piece was probably the present no. V, composed as a sight-reading test for the men (this time) in the Conservatoire examinations of July 1901.

Soon Fauré, or maybe his publisher Julien Hamelle, was thinking in terms of a larger collection, for the remaining manuscripts of the collection show the revised title *Petites pièces pour piano*. Burrowing among old papers in summer 1902, Fauré found two fugues dating from his adolescent years, one of which he had already reworked in the late 1870s for his friends the Clerc family;[1] with a few more retouches these became the present nos III and VI. (The parallel fifths that occur in both fugues attest to Fauré's disdain for pedantry, and doubtless delighted his student Maurice Ravel. The two pieces' respective bar-counts, incidentally, make interesting comparison). Fauré then embarked on nos. VII and IV, whose manuscripts are dated respectively 2 and 27 August 1902, to complete what he thought would be seven *Petites pièces*. The dates, along with one or two other indications, suggest that he may have envisaged no. IV as the finale; his later *Préludes* end in a similarly sombre mood.

No. VIII took him by surprise, as we read towards the end of a letter Fauré wrote to Edgard Hamelle (Julien's son and business partner) from Béziers on 14 August 1902: 'I have an eighth *petite pièce* which is making my brain itch! If it works out, I'll give it to you as part of the bargain.'[2] A surviving sketch of just bars 11–14 suggests that this bell-like evocation was the piece's germinal idea. Such distinct allusions are quite rare in Fauré, though he admitted to having been similarly inspired by the pealing of bells for the third movement of his Second Piano Quartet. Despite Fauré's typical open-handedness in offering Hamelle the eighth *Pièce brève* free, the earlier part of his letter quoted above betrays a bone of contention with Hamelle, who had the habit of pressing picturesque titles on Fauré's music to try and boost sales. Fauré writes:

> I'd really like to have 600 francs for the four new pieces,[3] the last of which I'll bring you on my return [to Paris ...] I assure you it was impossible to give these pieces individual titles, and I'm convinced that in the present musical climate it's no longer necessary. The title 'piece' is perfectly accepted and a number is all that's needed to identify it. There are plenty such works that haven't suffered from the absence of individual titles.
> [Added at the end as a postscriptum:] Saint-Saëns entirely agrees with what I say about titles.

The eighth piece was complete by 4 September and, with a final modification of overall title, the volume of eight *Pièces brèves* appeared from Hamelle in 1902, the pieces headed as Fauré had requested, just by numbers, plus a list of their keys on the volume's title page. The dedicatee (née Marguerite Villard) was a painter and music lover, as was her husband, a cousin of Fauré's former student Charles Kœchlin. On 18 April 1903 Ricardo Viñes premièred nos. II, IV, VII and VIII at a Parisian concert of the Société nationale de musique. Not long afterwards Fauré's relations with the firm of Hamelle, which had been strained for years, took a final dive, and the *Pièces brèves* turned out to be Fauré's last instrumental work to be published by Hamelle. (Fauré's later works were published by Schirmer, Heugel and Durand.)

Whether that final dive prompted or was precipitated by Hamelle's treatment of the *Pièces brèves* is now hard to establish. Around September 1904 Hamelle decided to market the eighth piece separately under the title '8me *Nocturne*', a ruse that effectively wrested him one more Nocturne from Fauré.[4] The fact that he did this with a piece Fauré had given him free was followed by probably a worse insult: for subsequent reprints Hamelle added gratuitous titles above all the *Pièces brèves*, of exactly the sort Fauré had vetoed in 1902.[5] The full extent of Hamelle's cynicism emerged some time later, when Roger-Ducasse happened to meet him and asked if he didn't regret having lost Fauré's custom. Tapping his pocket, Hamelle *père* replied, 'Couldn't give a stuff. I've got what sells.'[6]

The first of the *Pièces brèves* became a favourite of Fauré's younger son Philippe, who at the relatively tender age of seventeen (in 1906) decided to arrange it for violin and piano. Ten years later Fauré suggested nos. V, VII and VIII to the harpist Micheline Kahn as feasible for harp transcription, and sketched for her some indications of how it could be done.[7] Unfortunately his annotations are now lost, and none of these transcriptions, if they were ever realised, have been traced.

Besides their straightforward musical beauty, the *Pièces brèves* are remarkable for their blend of coherence and diversity. Spanning up to forty years of Fauré's composing life, they reflect the many facets of his long composing career, from the surprising assurance and intensity of his adolescence (nos. III and VI), through the concise grace and lyricism of nos. I, II, V, VII and VIII, to the starker severity of no. IV which presages later works like the Seventh and Ninth Barcarolles and Ninth Nocturne.

Editor's Note

Fauré's distaste for lethargic tempi or any kind of rhythmic sloppiness is well documented.[8] He was no more in favour of rushing, and many of his metronome indications judiciously guard against either extreme. Unfortunately the *Pièces brèves* are among a few of his works that show some implausible metronome markings, starting with '96' for no I (an obvious misprint of his written '69'), followed by a curious fixation with 72 or 76. In nos. III–V these markings are frankly unsustainable, and the pieces' *poco rit.* or *allargando* indications make sense only at a more flowing tempo. For no. V at least, it seems probable that 72 was an error for 92. With all this in mind, and to allow flexibility over large paragraphs in nos III and VI, the present edition appends some editorial suggestions in brackets alongside the source indications.[9]

In 1922 Fauré persuaded Hamelle to print a corrected edition, revised by himself with the help of his former pupil Roger-Ducasse, of the Nocturnes, Barcarolles and various other piano works Hamelle had originally published. The 'Eighth Nocturne' (a title Fauré by then accepted as a *fait accompli*) thus reappeared in 1924 with retouches of dynamics and nuances which were subsequently carried over to reprints of the *Pièces brèves*. These are incorporated here with the exception of the tempo heading, which the 1924 re-edition amended to *Adagio non troppo* while maintaining the original (for once plausible) metronome indication. From one of Fauré's letters, dated 23 July 1922, it emerges that the amended tempo heading was decided by Roger-Ducasse, following Fauré's advice that he wanted the piece 'to be very calm'.[10] While *Adagio non troppo* can make descriptive sense relative to the piece's larger melodic line, it risks heaviness if read against the accompanying figurations that first meet the pianist's eye. For that reason Fauré's original printed heading is retained here.[11]

Fauré's manuscripts confirm his distinction between ⸗ arpeggiando signs and ⸤ brackets (for example across bars 31–32 of no. VIII). Although the latter sign is often taken to mean non-arpeggiando (as well as indicating hand distribution), its presence over some wide spans (for example at no. IV bar 7) suggests that Fauré's intent may have been to keep any inevitable arpeggiations nimble on such chords. (He had average-sized hands, and recordings of his playing show him lightly arpeggiating most spans of a tenth, sometimes even of a ninth.) In some places discreet hand redistribution can help. The opening of no. III here follows the first edition's layout, but the Critical Commentary lists an earlier layout helpful for smaller hands. (The present layout makes bars 3–4 in the RH consistent with bars 5–6; it would also, as it happens, have let Fauré finish a cigarette as he played. This observation is not totally frivolous: Ravel once said exactly that about the one-handed accompaniment to his song *Ronsard à son âme*, and many of Fauré's manuscripts show cigarette burns.)

The present edition is based primarily on the 1902 first edition and the 1924 reprint of no. VIII, corrected as necessary from other sources, notably autographs regarding such details as the accurate placing of nuances. Editorial ties and slurs are printed ⌢; other editorial additions are placed in square brackets [ ]. Cautionary accidentals in parentheses ( ) come thus from the sources and are not editorial.

The editor thanks those who have allowed access to sources or helped in other ways: Dr Chris Banks and the music staff of the British Library, Marie-Christine Daudy of the Bibliothèque musicale at the Abbaye de Royaumont, the music staff of the Bibliothèque nationale de France (particularly Elisabeth Vilatte), the Médiathèque Hector Berlioz at the Paris Conservatoire, the Library of Congress, Washington, and the Archives nationales de France, Paris; Paul Keeling and Vicky Reed of Peters Edition; also Sylvia Kahan, Dominique Merlet, Charles Timbrell, and Jean-Michel Nectoux whose published researches and willing help have been indispensable. The editor gratefully acknowledges the support of an Arts and Humanities Research Board Fellowship at the Royal College of Music, London.

Roy Howat

[1] See *Gabriel Fauré, his life through his letters*, ed. Jean-Michel Nectoux, transl. J. A. Underwood, London, 1984, pp. 78 and 89. Though the earliest manuscripts of the two fugues are dated 1869, they may have originated as École Niedermeyer exercises from the early 1860s (see Jean-Michel Nectoux, *Gabriel Fauré, a musical life*, transl. Roger Nichols, Cambridge, 1991, p. 298).

[2] *Gabriel Fauré, Correspondence*, présentée et annotée par Jean-Michel Nectoux, Paris, 1980, p. 247.

[3] This doubtless signifies nos. III–IV and VI–VII; Fauré had evidently already concluded terms for the three 'Feuillets d'album'.

[4] The manuscript of this piece shows the added heading 'Prélude', not in Fauré's writing; we can only guess where and when that idea originated.

[5] The second printing of the *Pièces brèves* (c. 1904) shows just the added title '8me Nocturne' at the appropriate spot on the title page; subsequent reprints add the remaining titles. For the record, these are: 'Capriccio', 'Fantaisie', 'Fugue', 'Adagietto', 'Improvisation', 'Fugue' and 'Allégresse'.

[6] See Nectoux, *Gabriel Fauré, a musical life*, p. 275; both the translation there ('No skin off my nose') and the present one somewhat sanitise Hamelle's original French (see p. vi). Recent events have completed a happier circle, with Urtext publications by Editions Hamelle (now merged with Editions Heugel and Leduc) of the original version of Fauré's Requiem and a first European edition of the First Piano Quintet op. 89.

[7] *Gabriel Fauré, his life through his letters*, pp. 259–60 and 299.

[8] See Nectoux, *Gabriel Fauré, a musical life*, pp. 43, 45, 294 and 487–8. The various Peters editions of Fauré's *Pavane* op. 50 quote Sir Adrian Boult's recollections of Fauré playing the piece at a reported minimum ♩ = 100, with no hint of rallentando at the end.

[9] This procedure was Brahms's suggestion to Clara Schumann for editing Schumann's piano works, advice that Clara ignored in favour of tacitly overriding Schumann's indications with her own.

[10] *Gabriel Fauré, his life through his letters*, p. 323. The piece's maximum tempo is effectively dictated by the bell-like bars 11–14; were it not for that passage and its later reprise, one could easily be tempted to take the piece at a faster *allegretto*; see Critical Commentary for Fauré's earlier variant indications in that respect.

[11] Fauré's chronic indecision over tempo indications, a known topic of mirth among his friends, is visible from his cello *Romance* op. 69, initially headed *Adagio* in manuscript, then changed to *Andante* and finally printed *Andante quasi allegretto* – almost exactly the opposite sequence from the eighth *Pièce brève* (see Critical Commentary).

PRÉFACE

Les *Pièces brèves* de Fauré, bien qu'elles datent de ses grandes années, restent étonnamment peu jouées, pour des raisons qui n'ont rien à voir avec leur qualité musicale. Leur réputation a longtemps été ternie, avant tout, par quelques indications métronomiques peu plausibles (problème abordé dans la présente édition). Leur origine en tant que morceaux de déchiffrage, pour certaines, les rend légèrement plus faciles que beaucoup d'œuvres pour piano de Fauré, même si la plupart demandent l'étendue d'une main d'adulte, et elles sont une excellente introduction à la musique de piano de Fauré pour ceux qui ne connaissent pas encore les œuvres de plus grandes dimensions.

La taille, le titre et l'ordre du recueil ont d'abord pris forme de manière un peu fortuite. L'incitation première fut probablement l'épreuve de déchiffrage de deux pages en *mi* bémol que Fauré composa pour les candidats aux examens de fin d'année du Conservatoire de Paris en juillet 1899. (À cette époque, on estimait encore qu'il convenait de soumettre les hommes et les femmes à des épreuves distinctes.) Lorsque la pièce fut publiée dans *Le Figaro* du 29 juillet 1899, Fauré avait déjà cinquante-quatre ans, mais enseignait au Conservatoire depuis moins de trois ans. Pendant de nombreuses années, on l'avait jugé trop dangereusement moderne pour cette institution, dont – ironie de l'histoire – il devint directeur en 1905.

Le 3 février 1900, *Le Figaro* publia une autre pièce de Fauré, cette fois un *Feuillet d'album* inédit en *la* bémol majeur. Bien qu'il n'y fût pas question de projets pour cette pièce, ce doit être vers cette époque que Fauré rédigea une page de titre pour des « Feuillets d'album, pièces pour piano » en *la* bémol majeur et *mi* bémol majeur (les présents n⁰ˢ I et II dans l'ordre inverse). Le morceau en *mi* bémol majeur n'est autre que le morceau d'examen de 1899 agrandi à près de deux fois sa longueur primitive. (L'appendice montre ici la fin originale, nous laissant apprécier d'autant mieux les ajouts ultérieurs de Fauré, notamment les ravissantes modulations aux mesures 19-24.) Un peu plus tard, un « 3 » fut ajouté sur la page de titre manuscrite devant les mots « pièces pour piano » ; la troisième pièce non identifiée était probablement le présent n° V, composé comme épreuve de déchiffrage pour les hommes (cette fois) aux examens du Conservatoire de juillet 1901.

Fauré, à moins que ce ne soit son éditeur, Julien Hamelle, songeait bientôt à un recueil plus vaste, car les autres manuscrits du recueil comportent un titre révisé, *Petites pièces pour piano*. En fouillant dans de vieux papiers au cours de l'été 1902, Fauré trouva deux fugues qui dataient de son adolescence, dont une qu'il avait déjà retravaillée à la fin des années 1870 pour ses amis de la famille Clerc [1] ; avec quelques retouches supplémentaires, elles devinrent les actuels n⁰ˢ III et VI. (Les quintes parallèles qu'on trouve dans les deux fugues témoignent du mépris de Fauré pour la pédanterie, et ravirent sans doute son élève Maurice Ravel. Il est du reste intéressant de comparer le nombre de mesures des deux pièces.) Fauré se lança alors dans les n⁰ˢ VII et IV, dont les manuscrits sont datés respectivement du 2 et du 27 août 1902, pour achever ce qu'il pensait être une série de sept *Petites pièces*. Les dates, avec une ou deux autres indications, laissent à penser qu'il pourrait avoir envisagé le n° IV comme finale ; ses *Préludes* ultérieurs se terminent dans un climat sombre comparable.

Le n° VIII fut une surprise, ainsi qu'on l'apprend vers la fin d'une lettre que Fauré écrivit à Edgard Hamelle (fils et associé de Julien) de Béziers le 14 août 1902 : « J'ai une huitième petite pièce qui me *démange* le cerveau ! Si je la réussis je vous la donnerai pardessus le marché [2]. » Une esquisse qui subsiste des mesures 11-14 seulement semble indiquer que cette évocation de cloches était l'idée qui a servi de germe à la pièce. Les allusions distinctes de ce genre sont assez rares chez Fauré, encore qu'il ait reconnu avoir été inspiré par les sonneries de cloches pour le troisième mouvement de son Deuxième Quatuor avec piano. Malgré la générosité caractéristique dont fit preuve Fauré en offrant à Hamelle la huitième *Pièce brève* gracieusement, le début de sa lettre citée ci-dessus trahit également une pomme de discorde avec Hamelle, qui avait l'habitude de donner des titres pittoresques à la musique de Fauré pour essayer d'accroître les ventes. Fauré écrit :

> J'aimerais bien avoir pour les quatre pièces nouvelles [3] dont je vous remettrai la dernière dès mon retour [à Paris] 600f [...] Je vous assure qu'il était impossible de donner à ces morceaux des titres particuliers et je suis sûr qu'au point où en est la musique actuellement cela n'est plus nécessaire. Le titre « pièce » est parfaitement admis et il suffit d'un numéro pour la désigner. Il en existe beaucoup auxquelles l'absence de titre particulier n'a pas nui.
>
> [Ajouté en post-scriptum :] Saint-Saëns est tout à fait de mon avis pour ce que je vous dis des titres.

La huitième pièce fut achevée dès le 4 septembre, et, avec une dernière modification du titre global, le volume de huit *Pièces brèves* parut chez Hamelle en 1902, les pièces étant marquées comme Fauré l'avait demandé d'un simple numéro, avec une liste de leurs tonalités sur la page de titre du volume. La dédicataire (née Marguerite Villard) était peintre et amateur de musique, de même que son mari, un cousin de Charles Kœchlin, ancien élève de Fauré. Le 18 avril 1903, Ricardo Viñes créa les n⁰ˢ II, IV, VII et VIII lors d'un concert parisien de la Société nationale de musique. Peu de temps après, les relations de Fauré avec la firme d'Hamelle, tendues depuis des années, se détériorèrent définitivement, et les *Pièces brèves* se révèlèrent la dernière œuvre instrumentale de Fauré à être publiée chez Hamelle. (Ses œuvres ultérieures furent publiées chez Schirmer, Heugel et Durand.)

Il est maintenant difficile d'établir si la manière dont Hamelle traita les *Pièces brèves* provoqua ou précipita cette rupture. Vers septembre 1904, Hamelle décida de commercialiser la huitième pièce séparément sous le titre « 8ᵐᵉ Nocturne », ruse qui lui permit effectivement d'obtenir un Nocturne de plus de Fauré [4]. Le fait qu'il l'ait fait avec une pièce que Fauré lui avait donnée gratuitement fut suivi d'un affront encore pire : pour les réimpressions ultérieures, Hamelle ajouta des titres superflus au-dessus de toutes les *Pièces brèves*, précisément de la sorte à laquelle Fauré s'était opposé en 1902 [5]. Le cynisme d'Hamelle émergea dans toute son ampleur un peu plus tard, un jour que Roger-Ducasse le rencontra et lui demanda s'il ne regrettait pas d'avoir perdu Fauré. En se tapant sur la poche, Hamelle père répondit : « J'm'en fous, j'ai c'qui s'vend [6]. »

La première des *Pièces brèves* eut les faveurs du fils cadet de Fauré, Philippe, qui, dès l'âge de dix-sept ans (en 1906), décida de l'arranger pour violon et piano. Dix ans plus tard, Fauré confia à la harpiste Micheline Kahn que les n⁰ˢ V, VII et VIII se prêteraient à une transcription pour harpe et esquissa quelques indications sur la manière dont cela pouvait se faire [7]. Malheureusement, ses annotations sont aujourd'hui perdues, et aucune de ces transcriptions, si tant est qu'elles aient été jamais réalisées, n'a été retrouvée.

Outre leur simple beauté musicale, les *Pièces brèves* sont remarquables pour leur mélange de cohérence et de diversité. S'étendant sur quarante années de la longue carrière de compositeur de Fauré, elles en reflètent les nombreuses facettes, de l'assurance et de l'intensité surprenantes de son adolescence (n⁰ˢ III et VI), en passant par la grâce concise et le lyrisme des n⁰ˢ I, II, V, VII et VIII, à la sévérité plus dépouillée du n° IV, qui préfigure des œuvres ultérieures comme les Septième et Neuvième Barcarolles et le Neuvième Nocturne.

Note de l'éditeur

Fauré n'aimait pas les tempi léthargiques non plus qu'aucune espèce de négligence rythmique, comme l'attestent les documents [8]. Il n'était pas non plus partisan de la précipitation, et bon nombre de ses indications métronomiques mettent judicieusement en garde contre ces deux extrêmes. Malheureusement, les *Pièces brèves* sont parmi ses quelques œuvres qui comportent des indications métronomiques peu plausibles, à commencer par un improbable « 96 » pour le n° I (une évidente coquille de gravure pour le « 69 » écrit par Fauré), suivies d'une curieuse fixation sur 72 ou 76. Dans les n⁰ˢ III et IV, ces indications sont franchement intenables, et les indications *poco rit.* ou *allargando* ne prennent leur sens qu'à un tempo plus coulant. Pour le n° V, au moins, il semble que 72 soit une erreur pour 92. Pour toutes ces raisons, et pour permettre une certaine flexibilité dans les grandes sections des n⁰ˢ III et VI, la présente édition ajoute entre crochets quelques suggestions de l'éditeur à côté des indications des sources [9].

En 1922, Fauré persuada Hamelle d'imprimer une édition corrigée des Nocturnes, Barcarolles et diverses autres œuvres pour piano qu'Hamelle avait publiées à l'origine, révisée par lui-même avec l'aide de son ancien élève Roger-Ducasse. Le « Huitième Nocturne » (titre que Fauré accepta alors comme un fait accompli) reparut ainsi en 1924 avec des retouches dans les dynamiques et les nuances qui furent ensuite reportées dans les rééditions des *Pièces brèves*. Elles sont incorporées ici à l'exception de l'indication de tempo, que la réédition de 1924 corrigeait en *Adagio non troppo* tout en maintenant l'indication métronomique d'origine (pour une fois plausible). D'une des lettres de Fauré, datée du 23 juillet

1922, il ressort que la nouvelle indication de tempo est une décision de Roger-Ducasse, suivant le conseil de Fauré, qui voulait que la pièce soit « très tranquille [10] ». Si *Adagio non troppo* peut paraître sensé pour décrire la grande ligne mélodique de la pièce, on risque une certaine lourdeur si on la lit dans le contexte des figurations d'accompagnement qui frappent d'abord l'œil du pianiste. Pour cette raison, nous conservons ici l'indication imprimée originale de Fauré [11].

Les manuscrits de Fauré confirment la distinction soigneuse qu'il faisait entre signe d'arpeggiando ∫ et crochet [(par exemple, mesures 31-32 du n° VIII). Bien qu'on considère souvent que ce dernier signifie non-arpeggiando (outre qu'il indique une répartition des mains), sa présence au-dessus de certaines grandes extensions (par exemple au n° IV mesure 7) semble montrer que l'intention de Fauré était peut-être de garder leur agilité aux arpègements inévitables sur de tels accords. (Il avait des mains de taille moyenne, et les enregistrements de son jeu montrent qu'il arpégeait légèrement la plupart des extensions d'une dixième, et parfois même d'une neuvième.) À certains endroits, une discrète redistribution des mains peut aider. Le début du n° III suit ici la disposition de la première édition, mais le commentaire critique cite une disposition plus ancienne, plus facile pour les mains plus petites. (La présente disposition met les mesures 3-4 de la main droite en conformité avec les mesures 5-6 ; elle aurait également permis à Fauré de terminer sa cigarette en jouant. Cette observation n'est pas complètement frivole : c'est exactement ce que Ravel dit un jour à propos de l'accompagnement à une main de sa mélodie *Ronsard à son âme*, et de nombreux manuscrits de Fauré comportent des brûlures de cigarettes.)

La présente édition est fondée principalement sur la première édition de 1902 et la réimpression de 1924 du n° VIII, corrigées le cas échéant à partir d'autres sources, notamment les autographes pour des détails comme le placement précis des nuances. Les liaisons de prolongation et de phrasé de l'éditeur sont notées ⌢ ; les autres ajouts de l'éditeur sont entre crochets. Les accidents de précaution entre parenthèses proviennent donc des sources et ne sont pas de l'éditeur.

L'éditeur remercie tous ceux qui lui ont donné accès aux sources ou aidé d'autres manières : Chris Banks et le personnel musical de la British Library, Marie-Christine Daudy de la Bibliothèque musicale de l'abbaye de Royaumont, le personnel musical de la Bibliothèque nationale de France (en particulier Elisabeth Vilatte), la Médiathèque Hector Berlioz du Conservatoire de Paris, la Library of Congress, Washington, et les Archives nationales de France, Paris ; Paul Keeling et Vicky Reed (Peters Edition) ; ainsi que Sylvia Kahan, Dominique Merlet, Charles Timbrell et Jean-Michel Nectoux, dont les publications et l'aide ont été indispensables. L'éditeur a bénéficié du soutien d'un Arts and Humanities Research Board Fellowship au Royal College of Music, Londres.

Roy Howat
Traduction : Dennis Collins

[1] Voir *Gabriel Fauré, Correspondance*, présentée et annotée par Jean-Michel Nectoux, Paris, 1980, p. 79-80 et 91. Bien que les plus anciens manuscrits des deux fugues soient datés de 1869, elles ont probablement vu le jour comme exercices pour l'école Niedermeyer dès le début des années 1860 (voir Jean-Michel Nectoux, *Gabriel Fauré, les voix du clair-obscur*, Paris, 1990, p. 300).
[2] *Gabriel Fauré, Correspondance*, p. 247.
[3] Certainement les n°s III–IV et VI–VII ; Fauré avait à l'évidence déjà passé un accord pour les trois « Feuillets d'album ».
[4] Le manuscrit de cette pièce comporte le titre « Prélude » ajouté, mais non de l'écriture de Fauré ; on en est réduit à deviner où et quand cette idée est née.
[5] La deuxième impression des *Pièces brèves* (vers 1904) ne révèle que l'ajout du titre « 8ᵐᵉ Nocturne » à l'endroit approprié sur la page de titre : les réimpressions ultérieures ajoutent les titres restants : « Capriccio », « Fantaisie », « Fugue », « Adagietto », « Improvisation », « Fugue » et « Allégresse ».
[6] Voir Nectoux, *Gabriel Fauré, les voix du clair-obscur*, p. 280. Les événements récents ont pris un tour plus heureux, avec des éditions *Urtext* chez Hamelle (qui a maintenant fusionné avec Heugel et Leduc) de la version originale du *Requiem* de Fauré et une première édition européenne du Premier Quintette avec piano op. 89.
[7] *Gabriel Fauré, Correspondance*, p. 256-257 et 295-296.
[8] Voir Nectoux, *Gabriel Fauré, les voix du clair-obscur*, p. 67-69, 296 et 482-483. Les diverses éditions Peters de la *Pavane* op. 50 de Fauré citent les souvenirs de Sir Adrian Boult, selon qui Fauré jouait la pièce à ♩ = 100 au minimum, sans aucun *rallentando* à la fin.
[9] Brahms avait conseillé à Clara Schumann de procéder ainsi pour l'édition des œuvres pour piano de Schumann, conseil que Clara ne suivit pas, préférant remplacer les indications de Schumann par les siennes.
[10] *Gabriel Fauré, Correspondance*, p. 322. Le tempo maximum de la pièce est dicté en fait par les mesures 11-14, qui évoquent des cloches ; s'il n'y avait ce passage et ensuite sa reprise, on serait facilement tenté de prendre la pièce à un tempo *allegretto* plus rapide ; voir le commentaire critique pour les indications antérieures de Fauré sur ce point.
[11] L'indécision chronique de Fauré quant aux indications de tempo, sujet d'amusement notoire parmi ses amis, est visible dans sa *Romance* pour violoncelle op. 69, marquée à l'origine *Adagio* dans le manuscrit, indication changée en *Andante* et finalement en *Andante quasi allegretto* dans l'impression – succession qui est presque l'opposé exact de celle de la huitième *Pièce brève* (voir commentaire critique).

VORWORT

Faurés *Pièces brèves* entstammen einem guten Jahrgang, sind aber aus Gründen, die mit ihrer musikalischen Qualität nichts zu tun haben, immer noch erstaunlich selten zu hören. Vor allen Dingen hat ihr Ansehen lange unter diversen unerklärlichen Metronomangaben gelitten (ein Problem, das die vorliegende Ausgabe angegangen ist). Dass sie unter anderem als Übungsstücke zum Vom-Blatt-Spielen entstanden sind, macht sie ein wenig einfacher als viele andere Klavierwerke Faurés, auch wenn sie überwiegend der Spannweite einer Erwachsenenhand bedürfen, und sie eignen sich ausgezeichnet als Einführung in Faurés Klaviermusik für alle, die noch nicht mit den umfangreicheren Stücken vertraut sind.

Umfang, Titel und Abfolge der Sammlung nahmen erst nach und nach ein wenig planlos Gestalt an. Der erste Anreiz war vermutlich Faurés Komposition einer zweiseitigen Vom-Blatt-Leseübung in Es-Dur für die Teilnehmerinnen an den Jahresabschlussprüfungen des Pariser Conservatoire im Juli 1899. (Damals wurde as noch als schicklich erachtet, Männer und Frauen getrennt zu prüfen.) Als das Stück am 29. Juli 1899 in der Pariser Tageszeitung *Le Figaro* abgedruckt wurde, war Fauré bereits vierundfünfzig Jahre alt, gehörte aber erst seit drei Jahren dem Lehrkörper des Conservatoire an. Lange Jahre hatte er als zu gefährlich modern für diese Institution gegolten, als deren Direktor er ironischerweise im Jahr 1905 berufen wurde.

Am 3. Februar 1900 brachte *Le Figaro* erneut ein Stück von Fauré, und zwar diesmal ein unveröffentlichtes *Feuillet d'album* in As-Dur. Was er mit dem Stück vorhatte, wird dort nicht erwähnt, aber es muss um diese Zeit gewesen sein, dass Fauré ein Titelblatt für „*Feuillets d'album, pièces pour piano*" in As-Dur und Es-Dur (Nr.

I und II dieser Ausgabe in umgekehrter Reihenfolge) entwarf. Das Stück in Es-Dur ist kein anderes als das Prüfungsstück von 1899, auf fast das Doppelte seiner ursprünglichen Länge erweitert. (Der vorliegende Anhang zeigt den Originalschluss, so dass wir Faurés spätere Ergänzungen umso besser zu würdigen wissen, nicht zuletzt die hinreißenden Modulationen der Takte 19–24.) Einige Zeit später hat jemand auf dem Titelblatt des Manuskripts mit Bleistift die Ziffer „3" vor die Worte „pièces pour piano" geschrieben; das vorgesehene, aber nicht genannte dritte Stück war vermutlich die vorliegende Nr. V, komponiert als Stück zum Vom-Blatt-Spielen, diesmal für die männlichen Teilnehmer der Prüfungen am Conservatoire im Juli 1901.

Nicht lange danach trug sich Fauré oder vielleicht sein Verleger Julien Hamelle mit dem Gedanken an eine umfangreichere Zusammenstellung, denn die übrigen Manuskripte der Sammlung sind mit dem geänderten Titel *Petites pièces pour piano* versehen. Als er im Sommer 1902 in alten Papieren kramte, entdeckte Fauré zwei Fugen aus seiner Jugendzeit, von denen er eine in den späten 1870er-Jahren für die mit ihm befreundete Familie Clerc überarbeitet hatte;[1] mit einigen weiteren Retuschen wurden daraus die vorliegenden Stücke Nr. III und VI. (Die parallelen Quinten, die in beiden Fugen vorkommen, bezeugen Faurés Abneigung gegen Pedanterie und werden seinem Schüler Maurice Ravel zweifellos Vergnügen bereitet haben. Überaus interessant ist übrigens ein Vergleich der Taktzahlen beider Stücke.) Als nächstes machte sich Fauré an die Nr. VII und Nr. IV, deren Manuskripte auf den 2. bzw. 27 August 1902 datiert sind, um die ursprünglich von ihm vorgesehenen sieben *Petites pièces* zu vervollständigen. Die Daten sowie ein oder zwei andere Hinweise lassen darauf schließen, dass er sich die Nr. IV als Finale vorgestellt haben könnte; seine später erschienenen *Préludes* enden in ähnlich melancholischer Stimmung.

Die Nr. VIII war, wie wir am Ende eines Briefes lesen, den Fauré am 14. August 1902 aus Béziers an Edgard Hamelle (Juliens Sohn und Geschäftspartner) geschrieben hat, eine Überraschung für ihn: „Ich habe ein achtes *petite pièce*, das mir das Gehirn kitzelt! Wenn etwas daraus wird, bekommt ihr es als Dreingabe zu unserer Abmachung."[2] Eine erhaltene Skizze der Takte 11–14 deutet darauf hin, dass der darin heraufbeschworene Glockenklang die Kernidee des Stücks war. Erkennbare Anklänge wie diese kommen bei Fauré recht selten vor, obwohl er selbst zugegeben hat, dass er sich für den dritten Satz seines Zweiten Klavierquartetts ebenfalls von Glockengeläut inspirieren lies. Trotz Faurés typischer Großzügigkeit, mit der er Hamelle das achte *pièce brève* kostenlos anbietet, verrät der erste Teil seines Briefes, dass es im Verhältnis zu Hamelle auch einen Streitpunkt gab, nämlich dessen Angewohnheit, Faurés Musik in dem Versuch, den Verkauf anzukurbeln, bildhafte Titel aufzudrängen. Fauré schreibt:

> Ich hätte gern 600 Francs für die vier neuen Stücke,[3] deren letztes ich Ihnen bei meiner Rückkehr [nach Paris] mitbringen werde. Ich versichere Ihnen, dass es unmöglich war, diesen Stücken individuelle Titel zu geben, und ich bin sicher, dass dies beim gegenwärtigen Klima in der Musikwelt auch nicht mehr nötig ist. Der Titel „pièce" wird ohne weiteres akzeptiert, und eine Ziffer genügt, um es näher zu bestimmen. Es gibt viele solcher Werke, denen die Abwesenheit des individuellen Titel nicht geschadet hat.
> [PS am Schluss des Briefs:] Saint-Saëns ist bezüglich dessen, was ich Ihnen über die Titel gesagt habe, vollkommen meiner Meinung.

Das achte Stück lag am 4. September fertig vor, und mit einer letzten Änderung des Obertitels erschien der Band der acht *Pièces brèves* 1902 bei Hamelle; die Stücke waren so überschrieben, wie es Fauré verlangt hatte, nur beziffert und mit einer Aufstellung der Tonarten auf dem Titelblatt des Bandes. Die Widmungsträgerin (geb. Marguerite Villard) war Malerin und Musikliebhaberin; ihr Mann, ebenfalls Maler und Musikenthusiast, war ein Cousin von Faurés ehemaligem Schüler Charles Kœchlin. Am 18. April 1903 gab Ricardo Viñes die Uraufführung der Nr. II, IV, VII und VIII anlässlich eines Konzerts der Société nationale de musique in Paris. Nicht lange danach ging es mit den Beziehungen Faurés zum Verlagshaus Hamelle, die seit Jahren gespannt waren, endgültig bergab, und die *Pièces brèves* erwiesen sich als Faurés letzte Instrumentalwerke, die von Hamelle herausgegeben wurden. (Die späteren Werke Faurés erschienen bei Schirmer, Heugel und Durand.)

Ob dieser endgültige Abbruch der Beziehungen durch Hamelles Umgang mit dem *Pièces brèves* ausgelöst oder beschleunigt wurde, ist aus heutiger Sicht schwer festzustellen. Etwa im September 1904 entschied Hamelle, das achte Stück getrennt unter dem Titel *8me Nocturne* zu vertreiben, eine List, die ihm im Endeffekt noch eine Nocturne von Fauré einbrachte.[4] Der Tatsache, dass er dies mit einem Stück tat, das Fauré ihm unentgeltlich zur Verfügung gestellt hatte, folgten noch schlimmere Beleidigungen: Aus Anlass späterer Nachdrucke fügte Hamelle sämtlichen *Pièces brèves* unnötige Titel genau jener Art hinzu, die sich Fauré 1902 verbeten hatte.[5] Das volle Ausmaß des Zynismus von Hamelle zeigte sich einige Zeit später, als ihn Roger-Ducasse bei einer Zufallsbegegnung fragte, ob er es nicht bedaure, Fauré als Geschäftspartner verloren zu haben. Darauf antwortete Hamelle *père*, indem er sich auf die Tasche klopfte: „Das schert mich nicht. Ich habe, was sich verkauft."[6]

Das erste der *Pièces brèves* wurde ein Lieblingsstück von Faurés jüngerem Sohn Philippe, der im relativ zarten Alter von siebzehn Jahren (1906) beschloss, es für Violine und Klavier zu bearbeiten. Zehn Jahre später schlug Fauré die Nr. V, VII und VIII der Harfenistin Micheline Kahn als zur Bearbeitung für Harfe geeignet vor und skizzierte für sie einige Vorschläge, wie dies zu bewerkstelligen war.[7] Leider sind seine Anmerkungen seither verloren gegangen, und keine der Bearbeitungen, falls sie je vorgenommen wurden, konnte ausfindig gemacht werden.

Abgesehen von ihrer schlichten musikalischen Schönheit bestechen die *Pièces brèves* durch ihre Mischung aus Geschlossenheit und Vielfalt. Über einen Zeitraum von rund vierzig Jahren entstanden, spiegeln sie die zahlreichen Facetten der langen Komponistenlaufbahn Faurés wider, von der erstaunlichen Selbstsicherheit und Eindringlichkeit seiner Jugendzeit (Nr. III und VI) über den prägnanten Charme und Lyrismus der Nr. I, II, V, VII, und VIII bis hin zum spröderen Ernst der Nr. IV, die auf spätere Werke wie die Siebte und Neunte Barcarolle sowie die Neunte Nocturne vorausweist.

Anmerkung des Herausgebers

Faurés Abneigung gegen lethargische Tempi bzw. rhythmische Schlamperei jeglicher Art ist hinreichend belegt.[8] Ebenso zuwider war ihm allzu große Hast, und viele seiner Metronomangaben hüten sich mit Bedacht vor beiden Extremen. Leider zählen die *Pièces brèves* zu den wenigen Werken Faurés, die einige unglaubhafte Metronomangaben aufweisen, angefangen mit „96" für die Nr. I (ein klarer Druckfehler für Faurés handschriftliche „69") und gefolgt von einer seltsamen Fixierung auf 72 oder 76. Bei Nr. III–IV sind diese Vorzeichnungen offen gesagt unhaltbar, und die Angaben *poco rit.* bzw. *allargando* in den Stücken sind nur bei einem fließenderen Tempo sinnvoll. Im Falle von Nr. V zumindest liegt es nahe, dass 72 ein Druckfehler für 92 war. Vor diesem Hintergrund, und um über weite Passagen in Nr. III und VI hinweg Flexibilität zu schaffen, stellt die vorliegende Ausgabe einige Vorschläge des Herausgebers in Klammern neben die Quellenangaben.[9]

Im Jahr 1922 überredete Fauré Hamelle, eine von ihm selbst unter Mithilfe seines ehemaligen Schülers Roger-Ducasse korrigierte Ausgabe der Nocturnes, Barcarolles und diverser anderer Klavierwerke zu veröffentlichen, deren Erstausgabe Hamelle besorgt hatte. Die „Achte Nocturne" (ein Titel, den Fauré inzwischen als *fait accompli* hinnahm) erschien daraufhin 1924 mit Retuschen an Dynamik und Nuancierung, die dann in Nachdrucke der *Pièces brèves* eingingen. Diese wurden hier übernommen, mit Ausnahme der Tempobezeichnung, die in der Neuausgabe von 1924 in *Adagio non troppo* geändert wurde, wobei man die ursprüngliche (und ausnahmsweise plausible) Metronomangabe beibehielt. Aus einem von Faurés Briefen (datiert vom 23. Juli 1922) geht hervor, das die Änderung der Tempobezeichnung von Roger-Ducasse beschlossen worden war, und zwar auf Faurés Auskunft hin, er wolle das Stück „sehr ruhig" gespielt haben.[10] Während *Adagio ma non troppo* als anschaulicher Begriff für die übergreifende Melodieführung des Stücks durchaus sinnvoll sein kann, birgt er das Risiko von Schwerfälligkeit, wenn er im Zusammenhang mit den Begleitfigurationen gesehen wird, die dem Pianisten zuerst ins Auge fallen. Aus diesem Grund wurde hier Faurés ursprünglich im Druck erschienene Bezeichnung beibehalten.[11]

Faurés Manuskripte belegen seine Unterscheidung zwischen } Arpeggiando-Zeichen und [Klammern (wie z.B. über die Takte 31/32 der Nr. VIII). Obwohl letzteres Zeichen (neben seiner Funktion bei der Handzuweisung) oft als *non arpeggiando* interpretiert wird, deutet sein Auftreten bei großen Spannen (wie in Nr. IV, Takt 7) darauf hin, dass Fauré die unvermeidliche Arpeggierung solcher Akkorde rasch ausgeführt wissen wollte. (Seine Hände waren von durchschnittlicher Größe, und Aufnahmen seines Spiels zeigen, dass er die meisten Dezimgriffe leicht arpeggierte, mitunter sogar Nonen.) An manchen Stellen kann eine vorsichtige Neuzuordnung der Hände helfen. Der Anfang von Nr. III folgt hier der Anlage der Erstausgabe, aber der Kritische Bericht führt eine ältere Aufteilung an, die kleineren Händen entgegenkommt. (In der vorliegenden Anlage entsprechen die Takte 3/4 den Takten 5/6; wie es sich trifft, würde sie es Fauré obendrein gestattet haben, beim Spielen eine Zigarette fertigzurauchen. Diese Bemerkung ist nicht ganz so unseriös, wie sie klingt: Ravel hat einmal genau das über die einhändige Begleitung zu seinem Lied *Ronsard à son âme* gesagt, und viele von Faurés Manuskripten weisen Brandflecken von Zigaretten auf.)

Die vorliegende Edition beruht in erster Linie auf der Erstausgabe von 1902 und dem Nachdruck von Nr. VIII aus dem Jahre 1924, wo notwendig korrigiert auf der Grundlage anderer Quellen (insbesondere Autographen) in Bezug auf Details wie die richtige Plazierung von Nuancen. Vom Herausgeber eingefügte Binde- und Legatobögen sind wie folgt dargestellt: ⌒ ; andere editorische Zusätze wurden in eckige Klammern [ ] gesetzt. Warnungsakzidentien in runden Klammern ( ) sind den Quellen entnommen und stammen demzufolge nicht vom Herausgeber.

Der Herausgeber ist all jenen zu Dank verpflichtet, die ihm Zugang zu Quellen gewährt oder auf andere Weise geholfen haben: Dr. Chris Banks und das Personal der Musikabteilung der British Library, Marie-Christine Daudy von der Bibliothèque musicale der Abbaye de Royaumont, das Personal der Musikabteilung der Bibliothèque nationale de France (insbesondere Elisabeth Vilatte), der Médiathèque Hector Berlioz am Pariser Konservatorium, der Library of Congress in Washington, und der Archives nationales de France, Paris; Paul Keeling und Vicky Reed (Edition Peters); außerdem Sylvia Kahan, Dominique Merlet, Charles Timbrell und Jean-Michel Nectoux, dessen veröffentlichte Untersuchungen und zuvorkommende Hilfe unentbehrlich waren. Der Herausgeber erkennt dankbar die Unterstützung an, die ihm durch eine Arts and Humanities Research Board Fellowship am Londoner Royal College of Music gewährt wurde.

Roy Howat
Übersetzung Anne Steeb/Bernd Müller

---

[1] Siehe *Gabriel Fauré, Correspondance*, présentée et annotée par Jean-Michel Nectoux, Paris 1980, S. 79–80 und 91. Zwar tragen die frühesten Manuskripte der beiden Fugen das Datum 1869, doch begannen sie ihr Dasein wohl in den frühen 1860er-Jahren als Kompositionsübungen für die Ecole Niedermeyer (siehe Jean-Michel Nectoux, *Gabriel Fauré, les voix du clair-obscur*, Paris 1990, S. 300).

[2] *Gabriel Fauré, Correspondance*, Paris 1980, S. 247.

[3] Damit sind zweifellos die Nr. III–IV und VI–VII gemeint; den Vertrag über die drei „Feuillets d'album" hatte Fauré offenbar schon abgeschlossen.

[4] Das Manuskript des Stücks zeigt den Zusatz „Prélude", jedoch nicht in Faurés Handschrift; wir können nur vermuten, wo und wann die Idee entstanden ist.

[5] Die zweite Auflage der *Pièces brèves* (um 1904) enthält nur den zusätzlichen Titel „8me Nocturne" an der entsprechenden Stelle auf der Titelseite; in späteren Nachdrucken kommen die übrigen Titel hinzu. Der Vollständigkeit halber seien sie hier genannt: „Capriccio", „Fantaisie", „Fugue", „Adagietto", „Improvisation", „Fugue" und „Allégresse".

[6] Siehe Nectoux, *Gabriel Fauré, les voix du clair-obscur*, S. 280; die obige Übersetzung entschärft Hamelles Äußerung ein wenig (siehe S. vi). In neuerer Zeit hat sich ein glücklicherer Kreis geschlossen, mit Urtext-Ausgaben der Editions Hamelle (heute mit den Editions Heugel und Leduc zusammengeschlossen) der Originalfassung von Faurés *Requiem* und einer europäischen Erstausgabe des Ersten Klavierquintetts op. 89.

[7] Siehe Nectoux, *Gabriel Fauré, Correspondance*, S. 256–7 und 295–6.

[8] Siehe Nectoux, *Gabriel Fauré, les voix du clair-obscur*, S. 67–69, 296 und 482–3. Die diversen Peters-Ausgaben von Faurés *Pavane* op. 50 zitieren Sir Adrian Boults Erinnerungen, denen zufolge Fauré das Stück mit mindestens ♩ = 100 gespielt hat, ohne jeden Anflug von *Rallentando* am Schluss.

[9] Dieses Vorgehen hat Brahms Clara Schumann für die Herausgabe von Robert Schumanns Klavierwerken vorgeschlagen, ein Rat, den Clara missachtet und statt dessen Schumanns Angaben stillschweigend durch ihre eigenen ersetzt hat.

[10] *Gabriel Fauré, Correspondance*, S. 322. Das maximale Tempo des Stücks wird im Endeffekt von den glockenartigen Takten 11–14 bestimmt; gäbe es diese Passage und ihre spätere Reprise nicht, könnte man versucht sein, das Stück in schnellerem *allegretto* anzugehen; siehe die Anmerkung im Kritischen Bericht zu Faurés früheren abweichenden Angaben in dieser Hinsicht.

[11] Faurés chronische Unentschlossenheit in Bezug auf Tempoangaben, die bei seinen Freunden bekanntlich immer wieder Heiterkeit auslöste, ist aus seiner *Romance* für Cello op. 69 ersichtlich, die im Manuskript ursprünglich mit *Adagio* überschrieben war, was dann in *Andante* geändert wurden, um im Druck als *Andante quasi allegretto* zu erscheinen – fast genau die umgekehrte Reihenfolge wie beim achten *Pièce brève* (siehe den Kritischen Bericht).

Pièces brèves pour piano, Op. 84

À Madame Jean-Léonard Kœchlin

Gabriel Fauré
(1845–1924)

I

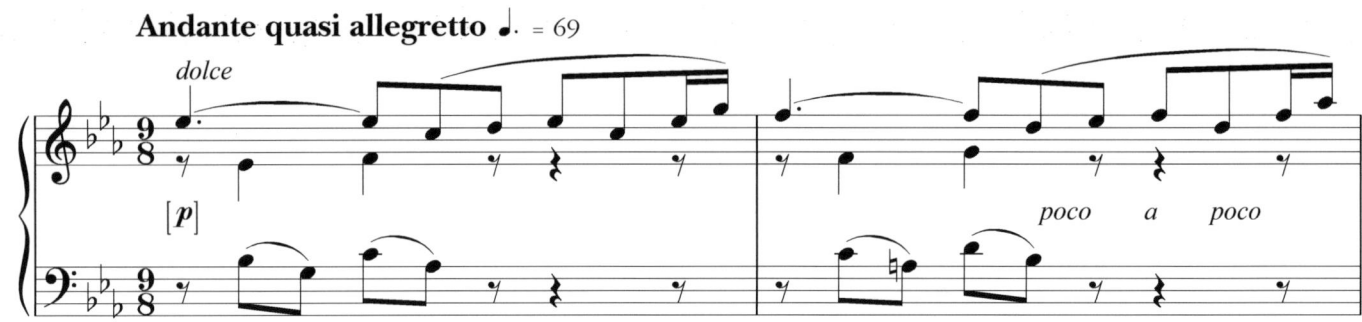

Edition Peters No. 7601
© Copyright 2003 by Hinrichsen Edition, Peters Edition Ltd, London

II

(1) Regarding tempi see Preface   Sur le tempo, voir Préface   Bezüglich des Tempos, vgl. Vorwort

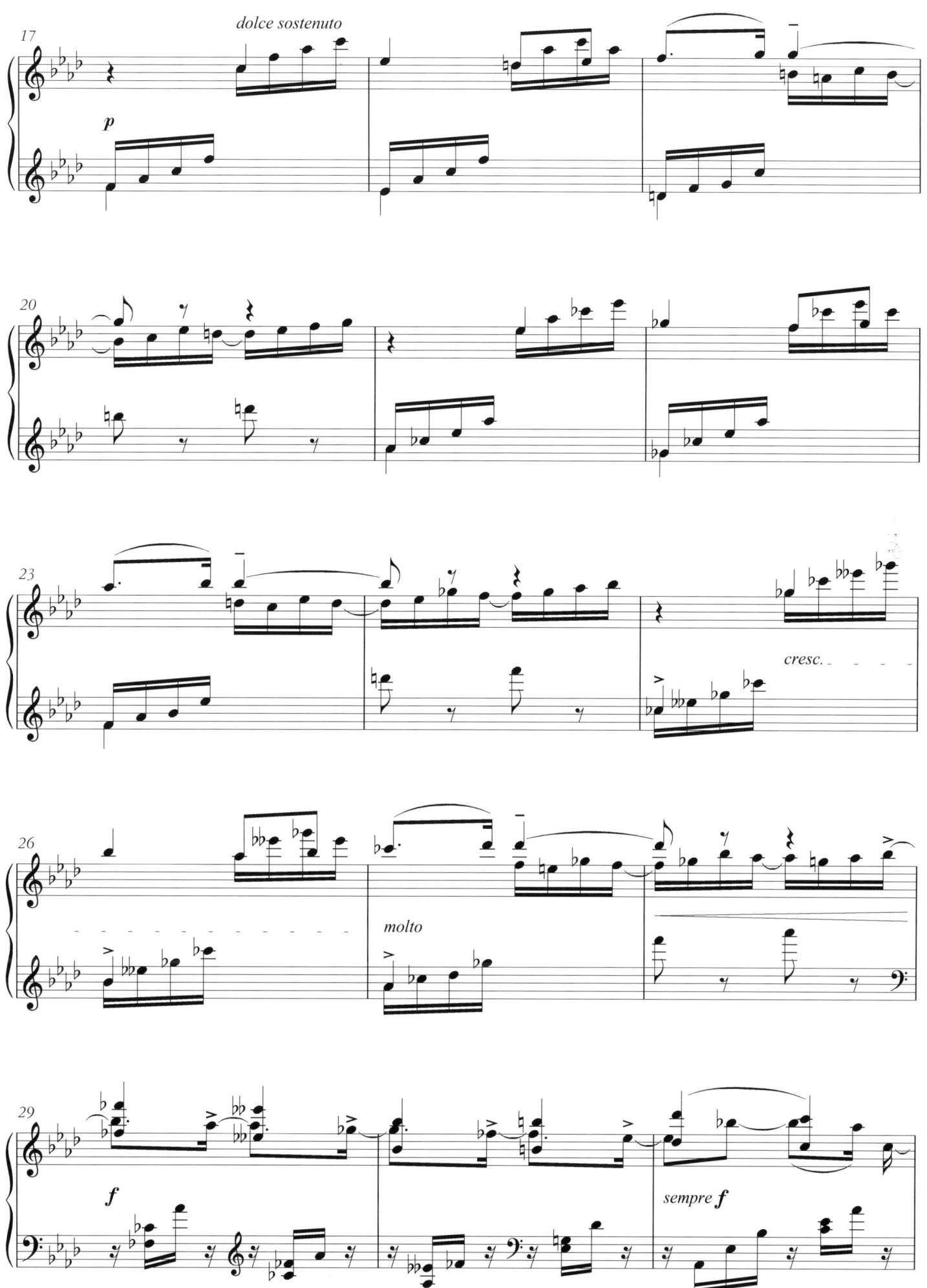

III

V

VI

VII

(1) Possibly *e'* intended; cf. bar 14   *mi* peut-être voulu; voir mesure 14   *e'* möglicherweise so vorgesehen; vgl. Takt 14

(1) Possibly *d* intended; cf. bars 19–20   *ré* peut-être voulu; voir mesures 19 et 20   *d* möglicherweise so vorgesehen; vgl. Takte 19–20

(1)VIII

(1) Also known as 8ᵉ Nocturne; see Preface   Également connu sous le nom de 8ᵉ Nocturne; voir Préface   Auch bekannt als 8ᵉ Nocturne; siehe Vorwort

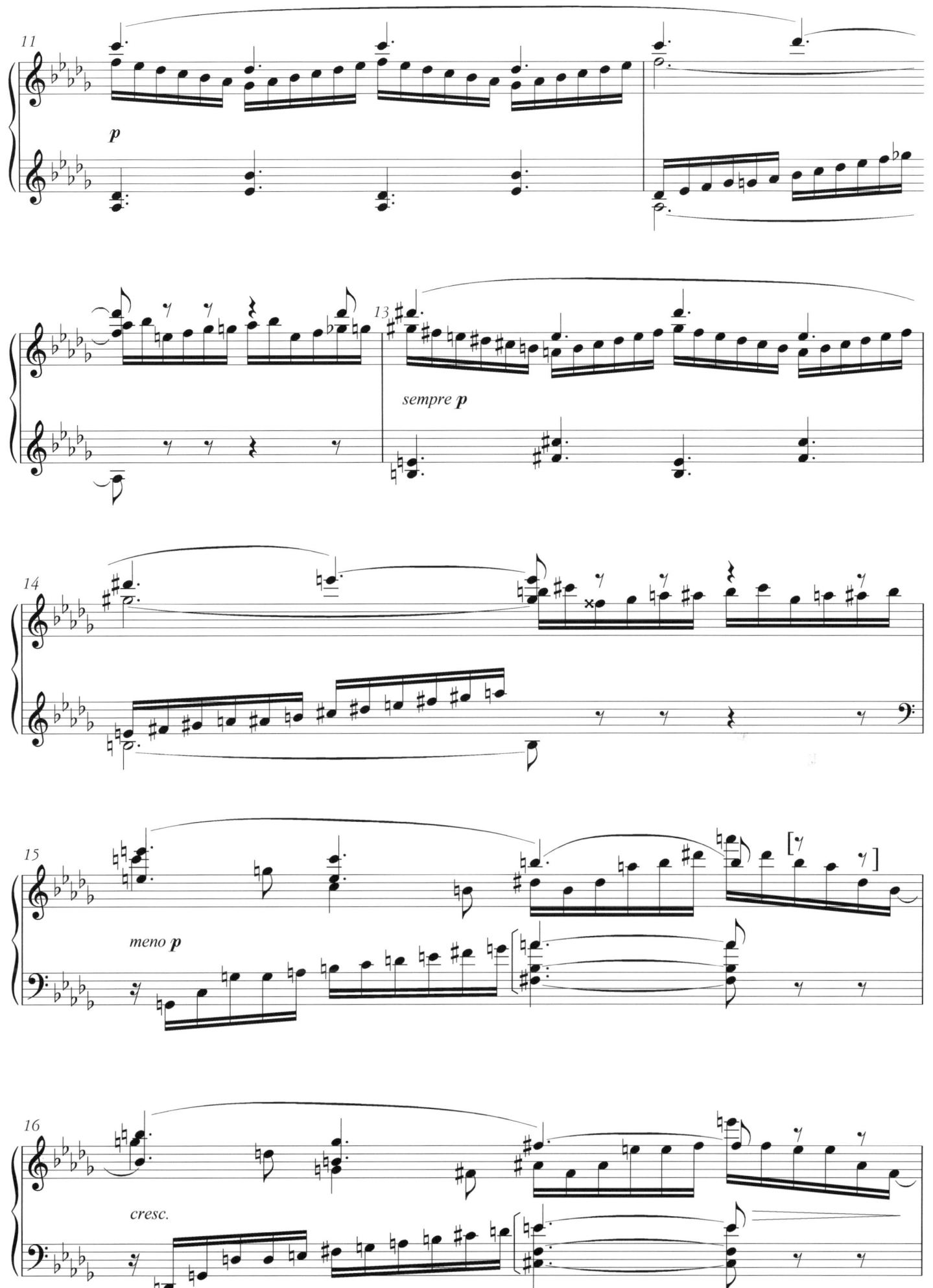

CRITICAL COMMENTARY

General editorial procedure and source priority are described in the Preface, **Editor's Note**. Minor oversights in only one subsidiary source (such as the occasional missing staccato dot or accent in a feuilleton print) are passed over in silence unless they involve a larger problem. Early reprints of the first edition that merely add Hamelle's titles (see Preface) are passed over in silence here, as they involve no musical changes.

RH = right hand
LH = left hand

Sources

I

A: Autograph manuscript used for engraving **E** below: Library of Congress, Washington, ML31.H43a / No. 64 Case (Music 1235). The cover page has the autograph dedication followed by 'Feuillets d'album / pièces pour piano / N° I (en la bémol) / N° 2 (en mi ♭)', with a pencilled '3' later added in front of the word 'pièces'. Above the first musical system is 'N° I', with 'I' then amended to '2'; the end of the piece is followed by Fauré's signature.

E: First edition, J. Hamelle, Paris, 1902 (J. 4897 H.)

F: Feuilleton publication of the piece as above, supplement to *L'illustration*, no. 3253, 1 July 1905. The piece is headed '*Pièce brève* / Pour Piano / GABRIEL FAURÉ, Op. 84', but with no mention of the rest of the collection; at the end M. Hamelle is merely acknowledged as publisher and copyright owner.

Secondary sources

A': Autograph manuscript of the original (shorter) version: Paris, Archives nationales de France, Aj^{37} 200, 2. The title page has the non-autograph information '1899 / Concours de piano (F) / G. Fauré', with an additional note on top right, 'publié Figaro'; the end of the piece is followed by Fauré's signature.

C': Non-autograph copy of **A'** (unidentified hand): Archives nationales de France, Aj^{37} 200, 2. This copy was doubtless for use of Conservatoire examination candidates in July 1899; the title page has 'Piano. F. / Concours = Juillet 1899.', again with 'Publié Figaro' added on top right.

F': Feuilleton publication of the shorter version as in **A'**: *Le Figaro*, 29 July 1899; part of *Le Figaro*'s annual publication of the Paris Conservatoire's end-of-year piano sight-reading examination pieces.

II

A: Autograph manuscript used for engraving both **F** and **E** below (showing two corresponding sets of engraver's marks): Paris, Bibliothèque nationale de France, Music dept, Ms. 20802 (dépôt Eric Bruneau / Editions Hamelle). The cover page has the autograph heading 'Feuillets d'album / (3 pièces pour piano) / N° 2', with '2' then amended to '1'; above the first musical system similarly appears 'Feuillets d'album N° 2 1'; the end of the piece is followed by Fauré's signature.

F: Feuilleton publication, *Le Figaro*, 3 February 1900, headed 'FEUILLET D'ALBUM / Pièce inédite pour Piano de / Gabriel Fauré'

E: First edition, J. Hamelle, Paris, 1902 (J. 4898 H.)

III

A1: Early autograph manuscript: Bibliothèque nationale de France, Music dept, Ms. 20296 (former Clerc archives). From Fauré's letters to Mme Clerc, the manuscript can be dated to between September 1878 and 2nd July 1879.[1] The title page is headed 'Petite Fugue' by Fauré, whose signature appears at the end. Structurally similar to the final version, this version shows minor variants of texture and dynamics, passed over here in silence except for larger variants towards the end, shown in the Appendix. An earlier autograph dated 30 June 1869 appears to be presently inaccessible, along with an autograph of no. VI dated 30 November 1869 (former Leyritz collection).[2]

A2: Autograph manuscript used for engraving **E** below: private collection, France. There is no cover page; the first musical system has the autograph heading 'Petites Pièces pour Piano / III', with 'la mineur' added farther left in another hand; the final system is followed by the autograph date '5 juillet 1902' and Fauré's signature.

E: First edition, J. Hamelle, Paris, 1902 (J. 4899 H.)

IV

A: Autograph manuscript used for engraving **E** below: Bibliothèque François Lang, Royaumont, Réserve 23. A cover page and inner title page show the autograph information 'petites pièces pour piano / N° 4', in the former case under a pencilled non-autograph addition 'Gabriel Fauré Pièces brèves / mi mineur'. Above the first musical system the non-autograph pencilled heading 'IV' is surmounted by a question mark; the end of the piece is followed by the autograph date '27 août 1902' and Fauré's signature.

E: First edition, J. Hamelle, Paris, 1902 (J. 4900 H.).
See Appendix regarding a related sketch, possibly not envisioned for piano, in one of Fauré's pocket sketchbooks, Bibliothèque nationale de France, Music dept, Ms. 17787 (3).

V

A: Autograph manuscript: Archives nationales de France, Aj^{37} 200, 2. The title page reads, non-autograph, 'Piano — Hommes / concours 1901'; the end of the piece is followed by Fauré's signature and the date '9 juillet 1901'.

C: Non-autograph copy (unidentified hand): Archives nationales de France, Aj^{37} 200, 2, presumably used by Conservatoire examination candidates; the title page has the information 'Piano. H / Concours = Juillet 1901'. Although neither **A** nor **C** shows engraver's marks, **C** appears to been have part of the source chain that led via **F1** to **E**, a relevant observation because some variants in **C** suggest pedantry on the copyist's part.

F1: Feuilleton publication, *Le Figaro*, 26 July 1901, as part of *Le Figaro*'s annual publication of the Paris Conservatoire's end-of-year piano sight-reading examination pieces from that month.

F2: Similar feuilleton publication (different engraving), *Le Monde musical*, 30 August 1901.

E: Edition by J. Hamelle, Paris, 1902 (J. 4901 H.) Source concordances suggest that **C**, or a now-lost derivative, served as source for **F1** which in turn served as source for **E**; **F2** mostly follows **F1** but includes a few details otherwise unique to **A**.

VI

A: Autograph manuscript used for engraving E below: Bibliothèque nationale de France, Music dept, Rés. Vma ms.504. The title page has the autograph information 'petites pièces pour piano / N° 6'. Regarding an earlier autograph dated 1869, presently inaccessible, see above under no. III.
E: First edition, J. Hamelle, Paris, 1902 (J. 4902 H.)
F: Feuilleton publication: album supplement to *Musica*, no. 77, February 1909 (issue devoted to Fauré); headed 'FUGUE / (EXTRAIT DE PIÈCES BRÈVES)', under the comment '*Morceau d'exécution assez difficile*'.

VII

E: First edition, J. Hamelle, Paris, 1902 (J. 4903 H.)
F1: Feuilleton publication: *Le Figaro*, 28 February 1903, headed 'Nouvelle composition de GABRIEL FAURÉ / « PIÈCES BRÈVES » pour piano / – VII –'.
F2: Feuilleton publication: album supplement to *Musica*, no. 52, January 1907, headed 'PIÈCE BRÈVE / (N° VII)' under the comment '*Morceau d'exécution difficile, de la plus délicate et de la plus pure musicalité*'.

The autograph of this piece, dated 2 August 1902, is unlocated since its appearance in the sale catalogue for 29–30 April 1957 (lot 314) of the Geneva dealer Nicholas Rauch (information kindly supplied by Jean-Michel Nectoux).

VIII

A: Autograph manuscript used for engraving E1 below: Bibliothèque François Lang, Royaumont, Réserve 23. A cover and inner title page show the autograph information 'Pièces pour piano / N° 8', in the latter case under an erased non-autograph pencil annotation 'Prélude'. On the outer cover page another hand, doubtless Hamelle's, has added 'très pressé — tirer 2 épreuves au plus tôt — Ne pas tirer 2 épreuves de l'autre morceau (n°7)'. High above the first musical system is pencilled 'ré♭', and the end of the piece is followed by the autograph date '4 septembre 1902' and Fauré's signature. An additional page of abandoned fair copy contains a deleted version of bar 1.
E1: First edition, J. Hamelle, Paris, 1902 (J. 4904 H.)
E2: Revised reprint of E1, Hamelle [1924], as a revised reprint of the Eighth Nocturne, then incorporated into reprints of the *Pièces brèves*.
S: Fragmentary sketch on pages [4–5] of one of Fauré's surviving pocket sketchbooks: Bibliothèque nationale de France, Music dept, Ms. 17787 (5). The sketch consists of the present bar 11 to bar 14 beat 2, identical pitch-wise with the final text except for some incomplete RH notation in bars 3 and 4.

Variants and Remarks

I

Bar 1. E and F print metronome indication as ♩. = 96, all other sources give it as 69 (**A'**, **C'** and **F'** all read *Andante moderato* ♩[*sic*] = 69)
Bars 2–4. **A'** leads bar 2 RH slur past barline ending a system, with no completion at bar 3, then leads bar 3 RH slur to bar 4 note 1, with no following slur
Bar 4. **A'**, **C'** and **F'** start ⌐ immediately after *mf*; **F'** ends it at start of beat 3

Bar 5. A', **C'** and **F'** give upper staff as

A' and **C'** start beat 2 LH slur a note earlier **Bar 8.** **A** and **E** omit LH change to 𝄢 (ending a system or page in each case), present in **F**, **A'**, **C'** and **F'**. **F** starts *dimin.* at beat 2, **C'** at beat 2 quaver 3; in **A'** the word is written mostly inside ⌐, starting at beat 3
Bars 12, 15 and 17. **A'** and **C'** have an accent to LH note 1 ♩., as does **F'** at bars 12 and 17
Bar 13. RH slur in **A'**, **C'** and **F'** only
Bar 17. **A** and **F'** omit RH slur
Bar 17 onwards. See Appendix for reading in **A'**, **C'** and **F'**; the following comments for this piece involve only **A**, **E** and **F**
Bar 18. Beat 3 RH stemming as in **A** and **F**; in **E** the crotchet upstem also includes *b'♭*
Bar 20. RH♮ to note 4 and 𝄾 under note 9 present only in **A**
Bar 22. LH note 1 augmentation dot in **F** only; **A** omits ♮ to RH beat 2 *f'*
Bar 24. **A** starts ⌐ only at beat 3; present reading (as in **E** and **F**) suggests deliberate amendment to avoid overemphasis of semiquavers
Bar 26. All sources lead RH slur past barline ending a system, with no completion in bar 27; cf. note to bars 2–4
Bar 27. **A** gives RH beat 3 lower voice as

 (matching LH tenor motion)

Bars 29–30. Parentheses surrounding cautionary accidentals as in **A**; **E** and **F** misplace them round final RH accidental of bar 29 instead of bar 30, and omit them in bar 29 LH
Bar 32. ♭ to LH beat 2 *d'* in **F** only
Bar 34. **A** gives LH as:

and ties final RH *f''* over to bar 35 note 1 (omitting following RH slur)
Bars 35–36. RH lower voice phrasing as in **A**, **E** and **F** (unambiguous in **A**); the difference is left unchanged here as it makes for variety in performance
Bar 38. **E** omits *g'–g'* tie, present in **A** and **F**. **A** starts LH slur just after beat 2 *g*; **E** and **F** start it from *a*♮. **A** gives penultimate LH note as *c''* not *a'♭*
Bars 38–39. Pedalling in **E** and **F** only; **F** places the final ✽ almost a quaver earlier
Bars 39–40. **A** gives bar 39 beat 3 to bar 40 beat 1 as:

(the LH *b'♭* tied back to beat 1); **E** and **F** retain that tie as an apparent slur *b'♭–a'♭*, probably by oversight

II

Bar 4. RH stemming as in **E**; in **A** and **F** the 2nd upstem includes lower voice *f′*

Bar 5. 1st LH slur in **A** and **F** only

Bars 9, 11 and 13. **E** starts each LH slur a note earlier (under RH dyad). **A** and **F** omit this slur in bar 13; in bars 9 and 11 **A** gives the slur as in present edition except in bar 9 ends it a note earlier, **F** gives it both times as in present edition but above the notes

Bars 10 and 12. **A** and **F** extend slur at bar 10 RH and bar 12 both staves to beat 2 note 1; **E** does likewise only at bar 12 RH, otherwise as present edition. The problem lies in whether to match bar 14 RH (where a break after *a″♭* would be ungainly) or bars 53–57; the reading in **E** relative to **A** and **F** suggests a decision at proof in favour of the latter

Bar 14. **A** and **F** start $>$ just after start of beat 2

Bars 17–28. All sources voice upper staff inversely to the present edition (with the main melody as the lower voice), with the semiquavers in bar 28 beat 2 exceptionally down-stemmed but still above the 𝄽. Apart from the continuity problem implied by that last detail, the source voicing causes visual and engraving congestion, notably with ties. In bars 25–26 the broken line between *cresc.* and *molto* is editorial

Bars 33 and 35. *Arpa* sign as in **A** and **F**; **E** takes it up only to *c″*

Bar 39. **E** prints *espressivo* and *marcato* as separate indications, the latter under the lower staff; **A** and **F** omit *marcato*

Bar 41. **F** omits beat 1 LH ♮ to *b*. In **A** the lower RH tie is effaced, probably by error in the course of other emendations

Bar 43. $>$ placed as in **A** and **F**; **E** prints it between the staves

Bar 45. Main RH slur as in **E**; **A** and **F** start it a note later

Bars 50–51. Upper RH slur in **E** only

Bars 52 and 54. RH articulation (dots and slur) in **E** only

Bar 53. **F** omits ♮ to 1st RH *a″* but visible signs remain of its earlier presence; possibly an engraver's well-meaning initiative (relative to LH)

Bar 57. **E** prints a tautological augmentation dot to the first RH *c‴*

Bar 60. **F**: ♯ not ♮ to LH beat 1 *e′*

Bars 61–62. LH accents in **E** only. At bar 61 beat 2 **E** stems *b♮* in the LH chord downwards to *g* instead of upwards to *d′♮* as in **F** (slightly unclear in **A**; cf. bar 62)

Bars 63–64. 𝄻𝄼. placed as in **A**; **E** and **F** align it under LH note 1

Bar 64. **A** leads LH slur almost to barline; **F** leads it to beat 1 dyad of bar 65

Bar 65. **E** omits beat 2 LH staccato dot, present in **A** and **F**

Bar 66. Pedal release in **A** only

III

Bars 1–5. **A1** gives tempo heading as *Moderato* (no metronome indication) and places the opening voice on the lower staff for bar 3 beats 1–2 and from bar 4 onwards

Bars 2, 4, 6 and similar. The rhythmic notation ♩. ♫ is taken from **A1**; **A2** and **E** notate this throughout as ♩‿♫, omitting the tie in bar 15 LH doubtless by oversight

Bars 19–20. Bar 19 ♮ to *c′* in **A1** only. Layout as in **A1**; **A2** and **E** place RH lower voice on lower staff for last notes of bar 19 and note 1 of bar 20

Bar 25. ♯ to beat 4 *f′* in **A1** only

Bar 28. RH stemming as in **A1**; **A2** and **E** stem lower notes 1–2 together with upper voice; cf. bar 29. **A2** and **E** give dynamics as *poco a poco cresc.*, editorially rephrased in view of bars 29–30

Bars 30 and 42. **A2** and **E** place *f* at last quaver of bars 29 and 41 (near the barline in **A2**), ending $<$ just before it, probably because of more restricted space in **A2**

Bar 32 onwards. See Appendix for reading in **A1**

Bar 43. **A2** includes the word *dimin.* inside the $>$; **E** prints *dim.* below it

Bar 46. All sources: *p* at beat 1 (redundant in **A2** and **E**). **E** prints grace note as F not A, probably the result of reading the grace note line in **A2** as a ledger line

IV

Bar 1. **A**: ♩ = [*sic*, no number specified]; **E**: (♩ = 72)

Bar 16. $>$ as in **A**: **E** prints it only from the penultimate to the last note

Bar 17. LH minim dyad stemmed as in **A**: **E** stems voices separately (cf. bars 16 and 18)

Bar 24. **A** and **E** stem LH beat 3 quavers downwards (restricted space in **A**); editorially inverted

Bar 27. **A** and **E** give LH beat 2 *b* as ♩ not ♪; editorially amended in line with bar 25 where **A** shows the same emendation

Bar 34. **A** omits LH augmentation dot, perhaps because of a preceding deleted version that compresses the present bars 34–36 into two bars, with *B′* starting beat 2

Bars 46, 48–50. **A** and **E** stem LH quavers downwards (restricted space in **A**); editorially inverted

V

Bars 2–4 and 10. Pedal releases up to bar 10 beat 2 placed as in **A**, the remaining one as in **F1–2** and **E** (**A** and **C** place it on beat 4, overlooking the LH leap necessary for most hands). Up to bar 10 beat 2 **E** places the pedal releases a quaver later than in present edition (under the quaver each time), possibly in overcompensation for **C** whose strong writing slant makes some of the indications lie somewhat left of their position in **A** (cf. note to bars 8–9). **F1–2** place the indications mostly as in **E**, with slight ambiguity in the direction of **A** and **C** which they follow at bar 3 and bar 4 beat 2. At bar 10 beat 3 **C** places 𝄻𝄼. under ♀; **A** has the indication both there and in the present position (other sources as present edition). Cf. other notes on pedal indications from bar 8 onwards

Bars 2, 4 and 10. Beat 4 RH articulation as in **A**; **C** has each slur but omits all dots; **F1** and **E** follow **C** except omit slur too at bar 4; **F** follows **A** except omits slur and dots in bar 4

Bar 4. **C** gives penultimate RH note as *e′* not *d′*, with later pencilled annotation 'd♯' [*sic*, not '*ré*'] above

Bars 5–7. **F1–2** and **E** end slur on last note of bar 5 (instead of a note later), likewise all sources on last note of bar 6. In **A** both these slurs originally tailed off ambiguously above the last note of bars 5 and 6 respectively, before the former of them (only) was extended as in present edition (and **C**)

Bars 6–8. Beaming as in **A** and **C**; **F1–2** and **E** beam LH to RH lower voice in bars 6–7 beats 1–2 and throughout bar 8. All sources supply a crotchet rest to each RH beat 3, as do **A** and **C** to each LH beat 4; **F1–2** print the latter in bar 8 only, **E** in bar 6 only

Bar 8. RH slur in **A** only

Bars 8–9. **C** places all but the last pedal indication quite far to the left, with the releases under or just after the 3rd semiquaver of each group (as also in **F1–2**), but then conversely aligns the final release under the RH *g′♯* at bar 9 beat 3

Bar 9. *p* in **A** and **C** only. **F1** omits 𝄪 to LH beat 1 *a*. LH beat 1 stemming as in **E**; **A** includes the 1st semiquaver in the crotchet downstem, as does **C** but not with complete clarity; **F1–2** conversely include *d♯* in the semiquaver upstem

Bar 15. All sources except **A** have a supplementary $<$ across this bar, probably because of a page change in **C**

Bars 17–19. Pedal releases up to bar 19 beat 3 aligned as in **F1** and **E**, except the first one in bar 18, which all sources place almost a note earlier than in the present edition; thereafter as in **A**. Up to bar 19 beat 2 **A** and **F2** place the releases almost a note earlier; at bar 19 beats 3–4 **F1** and **E** place them under the LH quaver, **F2** reading as **F1** and **E** at beat 3 but as **A** at beat 4. **C** reads ambiguously between the two versions up to bar 19 beat 2, then from beat 3 places the releases slightly farther left than even **F1–2** and **E** do. Cf. notes to bar 20 and bars 21, 23 etc.

Bar 18. LH as in **A**; **C** gives beat 3 note 2 as $c\sharp$ not e; **F1–2** and **E** do likewise with both notes 2 and 4 of beat 3

Bar 20. **A** aligns pedal releases under each RH γ, **C** places them under each 4th semiquaver, **F1–2** and **E** place them marginally right of their position in **C** but still left of the quaver chord; editorially adjusted

Bar 21. *Dolce* placed as in **A**; the other sources place it between the staves

Bars 21, 23, 25–26, 28. Pedalling as in **A**; **F1–2** and **E** align each pedal release under the last LH note or dyad or chord in each bar, except that **F1** and **E** omit it altogether in bar 26; **C** places them at beat 4 of bars 21, 23 and 25–26 (viable if repetitive) and towards the end of bar 28

Bar 22. p placed as in **A** and **C**; **F1–2** and **E** place it redundantly in mid-system. Pedal release as in **A**; **E** aligns it under $f'\sharp$, remaining sources slightly before it

Bar 24. Beats 1–2 RH articulation in **F2** only. **F1–2** and **E** start last RH slur from crotchet $b'\sharp$

Bar 25. pp placed as in **F2** (and implicitly in **A** where it appears immediately above lower staff), implying that it may be intended just for the arpeggio(s); other sources place it in mid-system

Bar 27. **F1** includes each $e\sharp$ in the LH downstems (as well as in the upstems)

VI

Bar 7. Sources stem beat 1 $\flat\ e'$ upwards not downwards

Bar 12. **E** and **F** stem LH voices together in beats 1–2; **A** shows the present stemming amended to read as in **E**, possibly because of lack of space above the b; cf. bar 13

Bars 15 and 25. LH stemming (except bar 25 beat 3) editorially inverted (restricted space in **A**)

Bars 30 and 32. **A**: f *sempre* instead of f, but omits the following $>$ at bar 30 and f *sempre* at bar 34

Bar 34. Stemming as in sources; polyphonic logic would suggest a separate downstem for the RH beat 1 crotchet $f'\natural$, but this might cause rhythmic confusion relative to the following e'

Bar 37. **A** includes the word *dimin.* inside the $>$; **E** and **F** place it under

Bars 42–44. **A** omits LH brackets and *Poco rit.*

VII

Bars 12 and 14. RH phrasing as in **F1–2**; **E** ends the slur a note earlier each time (on 3rd RH triplet semiquaver)

Bar 19. **F1** omits p (starting a new page)

Bar 28. **E** and **F1–2** end RH slur at note 1 (d''), starting a new system in **E**

Bar 37. LH beat 2 crotchet stem (in **E** and **F1–2**) feasibly a false start at stemming the semiquavers upwards in the now unlocated autograph; cf. the lack of a corresponding crotchet stem at bar 38 note 1, likewise bars 35–36

Bar 41. } in **F** only

Bar 42. LH slur in **F1–2** only

VIII

Bar 1. Tempo heading as in **E1**; in **A** this is followed by ~~quasi allegretto~~ (perhaps deleted because of the faster basic tempo of the similarly headed *pièce* no. I), **E2** has *Adagio non troppo*; all three sources have the present metronome indication

Bar 3. Tenuto dash to beat 3 in **E2** only

Bar 4. Beat 4 LH rests in **A** only

Bar 9. All sources: additional semiquaver upstem to note 1 instead of the present γ; cf. bars 7–8 and 23–27. Dynamics as in **E2**; **A** and **E1** have $<$ in place of *cresc. sempre*

Bars 9–10. **A** ends RH slur on last note of bar 9 ending a system, bar 10 slur completion as in present edition; **E1–2**: separate slur for each bar

Bar 10. All sources give beat 4 semiquaver 1 as f' not d'; in **A**, however, the lower ledger line (of the two) lies right on the top staff line, possibly a slip of the pen intended for deletion

Bars 11 and 13. Dynamics as in **E2**; **A** and **E1** have pp at bar 11 and *sempre* pp at bar 13

Bar 15. RH slur in **E2** only. RH beat 1 augmentation dots as in **A**; **E1–2** omit them and print one to the $c'\natural$ instead

Bars 15–16. Dynamics in **E2** only

Bar 17. Dynamics and nuances as in **E2**; **A** and **E1** have *meno* p instead of *mezzo* p and place *espressivo* between the staves (immediately after *meno* p in **E1**)

Bars 18–21. Dynamics as in **E2** except for bar 20 beat 4 where **E2** retains a redundant $>$ from earlier sources (editorially removed here); **A** and **E1** have *poco a poco cresc.* across bars 18–19, $<$ across bar 20 beats 1–2 to f at beat 3, $>$ across last two quavers of bar 20, no indication in bar 21

Bars 23–24. Dynamics as in **E1–2**; **A** has *meno* p at bar 23 and omits *sempre* at bar 24

Bars 29–31. Dynamics as in **E2**; **A** and **E1** have pp instead of p each time

Bars 31–32. LH tenuto dashes in **E2** only

Bar 32. **E1–2**: augmentation dots to LH chord, contradicting the following γ, probably engraver's confusion with bar 31

---

[1] *Gabriel Fauré, his life through his letters*, pp. 78 and 89.

[2] Dates according to Robert Orledge, *Gabriel Fauré*, London, 1979, p. 277.

APPENDIX

a: no. I, bar 17 onwards as in A', C' and F'

b: no. III, bar 32 onwards as in A'

c: sketch related to no. IV